D1527996

EXCELLENCE

God's Path to Promotion

Introduction to

Excellence
How to Pursue an Excellent Spirit

Andrew Wommack

Published in partnership between Andrew Wommack Ministries and Harrison House Publishers.

Woodland Park, CO 80863 – Shippensburg, PA 17257

ISBN 13 TP: 978-1-59548-718-6

ISBN 13 eBook: 978-1-6675-0931-0

For Worldwide Distribution, Printed in the USA

1 2 3 4 5 6 / 27 26 25 24

Contents

Introduction

Every one of us wants to excel. It's the way God made us. Whether we work for someone, have our own business, or want to reach more people through our ministry, we want to see growth. Being a person of excellence is not a state of being, but a state of mind. It's an attitude. It's a choice. In the Parable of the Talents, all but one servant multiplied the talents the master gave them to steward (Matt. 25:14-30). The faithful servants were promoted to take on greater responsibility, the unfaithful servant wasn't. Success or failure were not automatic, they were determined by the choices the servants made.

God created every person for greatness. If you work at a business, He wants you to be the best worker there. If you are a farmer, He wants to give you wisdom to grow better crops. If God has called you to be a parent, He wants to bless you so you can build a godly legacy. So, if God created every person for greatness, why isn't everyone successful?

I meet people all of the time who tell me, "You don't understand: It's the color of my skin, my lack of education, my gender . . . I'm being discriminated against." They have plenty of reasons to put a ceiling on their success. Not a single person has as many strikes against them as Daniel and his three friends had. Yet they chose to walk in a spirit of excellence that caused them to prosper (Dan. 1:17, 5:12-14, and 6:3). This is a principle found throughout Scripture: God promotes those with an excellent spirit. Look at Psalm 75:6-7:

> *For promotion* cometh *neither from the east, nor from the west, nor from the south. But God* is *the judge: he putteth down one, and setteth up another.*

You will see four qualities of an excellent spirit in the lives of Daniel, Hananiah, Mishael, and Azariah. (The last three are better known as Shadrach, Meshach, and Abednego.) If you live out these qualities in your own life, an excellent spirit will develop within you, and God will promote you. You'll have to be consistent, and it won't come without adversity and problems, but an excellent spirit will cause you to continually rise to the top. It will only be a matter of time!

Chapter 1

Hold on to Your Identity

We don't know the specific details of how Daniel obtained an excellent spirit. However, the Scriptures give us plenty of examples of what he did to maintain an excellent spirit, which draws a direct correlation to being promoted.

When God promotes a person, it's because they have an excellent spirit. The world will promote people simply based on externals. Even the prophet Samuel was tempted to anoint a man as king just based on his appearance, but the Lord said to him,

> *Look not on his countenance, or on the height of his stature; because I have refused him: for the LORD seeth not as man seeth; for man looketh on the outward appearance, but the Lord looketh on the heart.*

> 1 Samuel 16:7

Here, the word *heart* is not talking about the physical organ but your mental disposition, attitude, or spirit. In this passage, God was preparing to promote David to be king because he had an excellent spirit.

The first quality of an excellent spirit is the ability to hold on to your identity in Christ. When circumstances push the right buttons, many Christians struggle to maintain their identity.

Jesus spoke about this in Mark 4 when He said people will stumble when

> *affliction or persecution ariseth for the word's sake.*
>
> Mark 4:17b

You have to hold on to what God said about you if you're going to have an excellent spirit. As a Christian, you must have grit. You must have a tenacity that no matter what your circumstances are, you won't quit believing what God said about you.

This is one quality we see in Daniel and his three friends, Hananiah, Mishael, and Azariah. They dealt with adversity that most Christians could never even imagine, yet they maintained their identity. Here is a little background explaining what led to the challenges these young men faced.

The Israelites were a conquered people. Jerusalem was occupied. The entire nation of Israel was completely overrun in a Babylonian siege. Thousands of people were killed under Nebuchadnezzar, king of Babylon. Daniel and his friends probably saw their family members killed in front of them. After he'd carried out a successful campaign, Nebuchadnezzar's strategy was to find the educated people among the enslaved kingdom:

> *Children in whom was no blemish, but well favoured, and skilful in all wisdom, and cunning in knowledge, and understanding science, and such as had ability in them to stand in the king's palace, and whom they might teach the learning and the tongue of the Chaldeans. And the king appointed them a daily provision of the king's meat, and of the wine which he drank: so nourishing them three years, that at the end thereof they might stand before the king.*

> Daniel 1:4-5

Daniel and his three friends were chosen and put into a school where they learned the language of the Chaldeans. During this time, all their names were changed to Chaldean names: Belteshazzar (Daniel), Shadrach (Hananiah), Meshach (Mishael), and Abednego (Azariah). These names reflected the gods the Babylonians worshiped. The Chaldeans did this to strip their captives of their identity and assimilate them into their society.

After three years, these young men would appear before the king to be evaluated for their service to the Babylonians. Some would even be considered for positions of leadership. The average person today would be so bitter about what had been done to him, he wouldn't cooperate. But that's not the way these men looked at it. Even in the midst of terrible circumstances, they refused to change the way they saw themselves, making an impact on the man in charge of them:

> *Now God had brought Daniel into favour and tender love with the prince of the eunuchs.*

Daniel 1:9

This happened because Daniel kept a good attitude. Two other times scripture says there was an excellent spirit within him (Dan. 5:11-12 and 6:3). You see, circumstances don't change who you are; they *reveal* who you are. When you get to the place where you're not affected by what man does to you; then you'll hold on to your identity and not be distracted from serving God. At that point, you're beginning to develop an excellent spirit.

Submission vs. Obedience

These four Hebrew boys refused the king's meat and wine because it would have been contrary to God's commands (Lev. 11 and Deut. 14):

> *But Daniel* [and his friends] *purposed in his heart that he would not defile himself with the portion of the king's meat, nor with the wine which he drank: therefore he requested of the prince of the eunuchs that he might not defile himself.*

Daniel 1:8

Hebrews were not allowed to eat certain meats like pork and shellfish. Even if they were offered permissible meat, it needed to be prepared a certain way. We call it kosher today. Determined not to defile themselves with the king's provisions, these four Hebrews found a way to submit to earthly authority without disobeying God.

There is a difference between submission and obedience. Daniel and his friends submitted to their captors: they complied by learning the language and having their names changed, but they refused to eat meat strictly forbidden by God, choosing to obey God rather than man (Acts 5:29). Notice that they did it with a good attitude. This reveals that Daniel and his three friends refused to sell out! They submitted to their captors yet remained Hebrews at heart and stayed faithful to God.

In Ephesians 6:5-8 the Apostle Paul told slaves to obey their masters. Today you could say, "employees obey your employers". You need to serve your employer with a spirit of excellence—not only when he's looking, but continually doing God's will for your employer from your heart when you are alone. You must find your identity in Christ and refuse to surrender it, no matter what man does to you. That only comes from having a close, personal relationship with the Lord.

Be Transformed!

The verses the Lord first used to change my life in 1968 are Romans 12:1-2:

I beseech you therefore, brethren, by the mercies of God, that ye present your bodies a living sacrifice, holy, acceptable unto God, which is your reasonable service. And be not conformed to this world: but be ye transformed by the renewing of your mind, that ye may prove what is that good, and acceptable, and perfect, will of God.

In verse 2 it says, "*be not conformed to this world*". In other words, don't be poured into the mold of this world. Don't be like everybody else. Yet, this is the very thing most people do. They have a herd mentality, giving in to the pressure to conform. But if you want to be transformed, if you want to keep a firm grip on who you are in Christ, you have to renew your mind to what God's Word says about you.

The reason people are so quick to set aside who they are when facing challenges is because they haven't disciplined themselves to let the Word dominate their thinking. They're letting fear of rejection, demotion, or other negative consequences dominate them. They don't see God as their source. You need to find your identity in Christ and say, "God, it doesn't matter what anybody else does; I believe what Your Word says. You're my source." When you have this kind of relationship with the Lord, you'll hold on to your identity in Christ. You'll be able to function *in* the world, yet not be *of* the world. These are foundational elements of an excellent spirit.

Chapter 2

No Compromise

A person with an excellent spirit understands what to prioritize. They're able to make hard choices when challenges come. You see indications of this when Daniel and his friends are given pulse, or vegetables, instead of meat:

> So [Melzar] *consented to them in this matter, and proved them ten days. And at the end of ten days their countenances appeared fairer and fatter in flesh than all the children which did eat the portion of the king's meat. Thus Melzar took away the portion of their meat, and the wine that they should drink; and gave them pulse.*

> Daniel 1:14-16

Daniel and his friends had such favor and influence with Melzar, their overseer, that he consented to their request for vegetables. If you will stand for God, He will promote you. However, if you compromise, you'll fall for anything that comes along. You need to prioritize God's Word and establish your identity in Him by saying, "This is who I am, I will not deviate from it, even if it will cost me something."

The Language of the Devil

Compromise is a language of the devil. He will always try to trick you into sacrificing the truth to obtain a more favorable outcome (Gen. 3:1-6). He'll promise you whatever you want if you'll just take a shortcut (Matt. 4:1-11). Compromise, however, is not a characteristic of an excellent spirit. You've already learned that the first quality of an excellent spirit is having an identity rooted in God. The second quality is refusing to compromise that identity, no matter the cost.

Shadrach, Meshach, and Abednego refused to compromise. They could have been killed for it, but because they refused to compromise, their concerns were considered, and adjustments were made for them. They stood on what God's Word says.

You could say you need to be a person of conviction. You could say Daniel and his friends didn't fear man but instead feared God. Jesus said it this way:

> *How can ye believe, which receive honour one of another, and seek not the honour that* cometh *from God only?*

John 5:44

If you seek honor from people, you will wind up compromising. If you have a spirit of excellence, you won't allow yourself to be afraid of what man may do to you. You will choose to stand on your convictions and not compromise.

Into the Fiery Furnace

King Nebuchadnezzar had a golden statue of himself made and commanded that when the music played, everybody must bow down to the golden image or be thrown into a burning fiery furnace. Anybody who would build something like this and make people worship it has a serious ego problem. Shadrach, Meshach, and Abednego had a decision to make: Would they obey or disobey this order?

For the second time, the three Hebrew boys chose not to compromise. Again, this wasn't an attitude of rebellion against the king; they chose to align their lives with God's Word.

Nebuchadnezzar was furious when he found out Shadrach, Meshach, and Abednego would not obey his command:

Then Nebuchadnezzar in his rage and fury commanded to bring Shadrach, Meshach, and Abednego. Then they brought these men before the king. Nebuchadnezzar spake and said unto them, Is it true, O Shadrach, Meshach, and Abednego, do not ye serve my gods, nor worship the golden image which I have set up? Now if ye be ready that at what time ye hear the sound of the cornet, flute, harp, sackbut, psaltery, and dulcimer, and all kinds of musick, ye fall down and worship the image which I have made; well: but if ye worship not, ye shall be cast the same hour into the midst of a burning fiery furnace; and who is that God that shall deliver you out of my hands?

Daniel 3:13-15

What an arrogant statement. Nebuchadnezzar thought that no God was greater than him. He even challenged Shadrach, Meshach, and Abednego's God. God set the record straight! He just needed somebody willing to stand up and not compromise. God is looking for people with a spirit of excellence to flow through.

Many believers would love God to sovereignly change everything that isn't right, but that isn't how His kingdom works. It says in Ephesians 3:20:

> [God] *is able to do exceeding abundantly above all that we ask or think according to the power that worketh in us.*

It is important to remember God always flows through people. He's looking to show Himself strong on behalf of those who are loyal to Him (2 Chr. 16:9). When we ask, *Where is the God of Daniel?* God is asking, "Where are the Daniels of God? Where is the one with an excellent spirit, who will stand up like Shadrach, Meshach, and Abednego?"

So, Nebuchadnezzar brings Shadrach, Meshach, and Abednego before him and basically says, "I'll give you a second chance. If you will bow down now and worship my image, I'll let you live. If you don't, I'll throw you into a fiery furnace." Look at the answer they gave the king:

> *O Nebuchadnezzar, we are not careful to answer thee in this matter. If it be so, our God whom we serve is able to deliver us from the burning fiery furnace, and he will deliver us out of thine hand, O king. But if not, be it known unto thee, O king, that we will not serve thy gods, nor worship the golden image which thou hast set up.*
>
> Daniel 3:16b-18

"*We are not careful*" means they weren't full of care. They weren't afraid of the king. Their security was in God to such a degree that they valued pleasing Him more than they valued pleasing Nebuchadnezzar. You could say it this way: they feared God more than they feared man. They reverenced God and it emboldened them to stand firm and refuse to compromise.

When Nebuchadnezzar asked them who would deliver them from his hands, they essentially answered, "Our God is able to deliver us from this fiery furnace." But then they said something else that really reveals their uncompromising attitude. They basically said, "Even if God doesn't deliver us, we still won't bow down to your image." What a great stand! By this time, Shadrach, Meshach, and Abednego had been promoted to positions of authority in the Babylonian kingdom (Dan. 2:49). It would have been easy for them to justify a compromise and say, "We have to give in. It's to our advantage! If we don't, we will lose our position of influence." That is probably the predominant attitude of many Christians today.

However, because Shadrach, Meshach, and Abednego refused to compromise,

> *Then was Nebuchadnezzar full of fury, and the form of his visage was changed against Shadrach, Meshach, and Abednego.*

Daniel 3:19a

In other words, Nebuchadnezzar became so filled with fury that his whole face changed, like he was demon possessed. He was livid! If you start standing up for God and the truth, Satan will rally his entire kingdom against you trying to get you to compromise! Having an excellent spirit means you won't just "go with the flow". It will take effort to be like these young men, who purposed in their hearts not to defile themselves with the king's meat (Dan. 1:8). That's going against the current and swimming upstream. That is what God is looking for.

Whether God delivers you or not, you shouldn't compromise. That's a strong statement but this is what separates these men from most Christians. Many people today will only serve God if they know everything will work out to their advantage. If their bosses tell them they must compromise or be fired, if they're threatened with being thrown into prison for being Christians, they will do whatever it takes to save their own necks. You can't live that way and have an excellent spirit. You need to decide that if it costs you your job, freedom, or even your life, you will not compromise.

If you only look at how things will affect you in the natural, you're very short-sighted. It's been over 2,500 years since Shadrach, Meshach, and Abednego refused to compromise, and we're still talking about them. We don't know the name of one person who bowed to Nebuchadnezzar's image, but we know these young men because they put God first. We look at them as examples of how we should be. We'll always come out better in the long run if we refuse to compromise—if we fear God more than we fear man.

Nebuchadnezzar commanded the furnace be heated seven times more than normal and that the Hebrew boys be immediately thrown into it (Dan. 3:19). But when they were cast in, something happened:

> *Then Nebuchadnezzar the king was astonied, and rose up in haste, and spake, and said unto his counsellors, Did not we cast three men bound into the midst of the fire? They answered and said unto the king, True, O king. He answered and said, Lo, I see four men loose, walking in the midst of the fire, and they have no hurt; and the form of the fourth is like the Son of God.*

> Daniel 3:24-25

I believe this fourth man was a manifestation of Jesus before He came to earth in bodily form, that He was in the fire with Shadrach, Meshach, and Abednego. All the fire did was burn off the things that bound them. When Nebuchadnezzar saw that they were not harmed, he called for them to come out of the furnace (Dan. 3:26). After having them examined, the king noticed that this miracle went beyond their bodies not being burned in the fire: their clothes weren't burnt, their hair wasn't singed, and not even the smell of smoke was on them! Look how Nebuchadnezzar responded:

> Then *Nebuchadnezzar spake, and said, Blessed be the God of Shadrach, Meshach, and Abednego, who hath sent his angel, and delivered his servants that trusted in him, and have changed the king's word, and yielded their bodies, that they might not serve nor worship any god, except their own God. Therefore I make a decree, That every people, nation, and language, which speak any thing amiss against the God of Shadrach, Meshach, and Abednego, shall be cut in pieces, and their houses shall be made a dunghill: because there is no other God that can deliver after this sort. Then the king promoted Shadrach, Meshach, and Abednego, in the province of Babylon.*
>
> Daniel 3:28-30

Nebuchadnezzar started singing a different tune when he saw that he wasn't greater than God. He actually gave a command that anyone who didn't worship the God of the Hebrews should be killed and that their houses should be made into a dunghill. Then he again promoted Shadrach, Meshach, and Abednego, the very ones who had defied him. Everybody would love a testimony like this, but not everybody is willing to have an uncompromising attitude. You must start developing an excellent spirit.

How God Wants to Use You

God used Daniel, Shadrach, Meshach, and Abednego to bring one of the greatest kings of the known world to a place of humility. This came out of their refusal to compromise. Nebuchadnezzar actually became like an animal and, for seven years, ate grass like a cow. He lost his mind. After seven years, his reason returned to him, and God put him back on the throne. Then he began to acknowledge that promotion comes from the Lord (Psalm 75:6-7). He said it's God who rules in the heaven and gives the kingdoms to whomever He wants. Then Nebuchadnezzar made one of the strongest statements in the Bible:

Those that walk in pride he is able to abase.

Daniel 4:37b

God accomplished awesome things through Daniel and his friends. He wants to do awesome things through you too.

Later in Daniel, scripture says,

The people that do know their God shall be strong, and do exploits.

Daniel 11:32b

This doesn't happen for people who compromise. But if you begin to hold on to your identity in Christ, know Him on an intimate level, and refuse to compromise, He will use you!

Many people can't do what I've been sharing with you. They love their lives too much. But scripture says,

They overcame him by the blood of the Lamb, and by the word of their testimony; and they loved not their lives unto the death.

Revelation 12:11

Personally, I believe God for protection and that He will allow me to continue to minister. But if our nation continues to go the way that it's going, I may be censored or put in prison. I don't believe that's God's best, but I know that by serving Him, I will be persecuted.

For example, through our Truth & Liberty Coalition, I am able to freely comment on social and cultural issues from a biblical perspective. I believe as a minister of the Gospel, I have every right to speak from the Word of God about things like homosexuality, abortion, the ungodliness in our culture, and the way we see America going. But my staff created Truth & Liberty as a 501(c)4 organization to provide extra protection for our ministry.

For some time, we've had a Truth & Liberty television program where we talk about these things and interview the movers and shakers who are really making a difference in our nation. There are times when I speak on topics that may be controversial—and it causes no small stir!

As a matter of fact, there was a major online video platform that pulled a couple of episodes off the internet because of what we were saying. That's what is referred to as "cancel culture," where they silence people whose opinions offend them. It's trying to force people to be politically correct rather than speak the truth.

After that happened, my staff came to me and said, "You've been censored twice now, and if they censor you again within a certain period of time, they'll block you from their platform." Then they asked me, "Would you like to have those videos edited before we post them on the internet?"

That's when I told my staff, "If they want to censor me, that's one thing. But if *we* edit those videos, I would be censoring myself." And I wasn't about to do that! If I spoke from the truth of God's Word and that offended someone so much they would cancel me, I would consider it a badge of honor. I'm not going to deny someone else the opportunity to hear the truth because of what the consequences might be.

In another instance, during the pandemic response of 2020, the government declared that churches were nonessential and tried to stop people from worshiping. We even received a cease-and-desist letter during one of our events at Charis Bible College.

My ministry staff had a war room going nearly twenty-four hours a day, making plans in case the authorities came to arrest me. I even had people ask me, "What if they shut you down? What if they threaten to take away your 501c3 nonprofit status?" But worrying about what could happen to me is not how I live.

It's not my responsibility to consider what anyone else does. All I've got control over is myself. And I'm only going to do what God tells me to do. So, if they had put me in jail, that's their problem. I'd just start a jail ministry and get everybody in the jail saved! I'm not going to evaluate what God wants me to do based on what the consequences may be.

As it turned out, the State of Colorado sued us, and we sued them back. Eventually, the U.S. Supreme Court ruled in favor of churches in other states who fought back against lockdowns. And because of that, the State of Colorado backed down. During that time our income increased dramatically, more people became familiar with our ministry, and our impact with the Gospel grew. That's awesome!

At the time, I was one of the few ministers who stood up to the governor of Colorado. All across the state, churches were told they had to close because they weren't "essential." And yet, marijuana shops, liquor stores, and other ungodly businesses could stay open. At first, we canceled some things because we were trying to be good neighbors. But the Bible says that Christians should not forsake "*the assembling of ourselves together*" (Heb. 10:25), so we told the governor our *voluntary cooperation* was over!

Now, if all the pastors, just in the county around Charis Bible College, had stood with me, the government officials would have backed down immediately. We wouldn't have received cease-and-desist orders. I wouldn't have been threatened with arrest. But because our ministry stood nearly alone—and won—all those churches benefitted. Because we were willing to fight when everything looked like it was against us, the body of Christ won. Praise the Lord!

John Quincy Adams, the sixth president of the United States, is popularly believed to have said, "Duty is ours; results are God's." We should never debate doing what the Lord has instructed us to do because of a fear of what might happen.

The Bible says that those who desire to live godly in Christ will suffer persecution (2 Tim. 3:12). In Acts 12, Herod killed the Apostle James with the sword and then had the Apostle Peter put in prison. Peter was delivered from Herod, but deliverance from persecution is not guaranteed. You are guaranteed that if you live godly by holding on to your identity in Christ and refusing to compromise, you will be persecuted, but you will also develop an excellent spirit.

I have made the decision that I will do what's right whether I am delivered from persecution or not. I will stand against ungodliness, and I will not bend or bow. This is a spirit of excellence. Interestingly, my refusal to compromise has earned the respect of some who disagree with my beliefs. I think that's what happened with Nebuchadnezzar and the young Hebrew men. If you want these kinds of results, you need to start doing the same things they did.

Perhaps you sense that God has more for you than what you're experiencing. Maybe you're doing everything you know for success, but you've encountered roadblocks. You might be experiencing the temptation to change who you are and do things that aren't in your heart for the sake of promotion. I'm telling you, in the name of the Lord, don't do it! A spirit of excellence starts with being who God made you to be and not compromising. If you will do that, God will find a way to promote you. I really believe that.

Chapter 3

Boldly Stand

The wicked flee when no man pursueth: but the righteous are bold as a lion.

Proverbs 28:1

The wicked flee when there's not even a reason to flee. But those who are righteous in Christ will have a boldness that is like a lion's.

Boldness is a characteristic of having an excellent spirit, and it's the third quality I want to discuss. When you know the God of the universe loves you, and you talk with Him as a friend, it gives you boldness. You'll be able to say, "Who cares what anybody else thinks or says about me?"

Refusing to compromise requires boldness because you have to be able to stand for truth no matter the consequences. Facing the threat of death, Shadrach, Meshach, and Abednego had to be bold. Some Christians can't handle someone rolling their eyes at them or sighing when they speak. So, they prefer to keep silent to avoid risking persecution. But the scripture says if you run with the footmen and they tire you, what will you do when the horsemen come (Jer. 12:5)? Applying this principle, if you can't handle somebody simply rolling their eyes or calling you a fanatic, you'll never be able to stand when they threaten to throw you into a burning fiery furnace! These are some important truths that aren't being said very often.

We Christians need to toughen up. The boldness we require develops as we spend time with God. It causes us to lose our fear of man and stop being passive. This boldness sets us apart from others. Daniel, Shadrach, Meshach, and Abednego all took a stand. Even rewards and gifts couldn't sway them. That's why we know of them today.

In John 5, Jesus was talking to religious leaders who loved man's praises more than God's (John 12:42-43). He said they weren't able to believe if they were seeking honor from man and not seeking the honor that comes from God only (John 5:44). The majority of people today are in this state. They need other people's acceptance and approval, yet Jesus said that if you seek honor from others, you can't believe. You have to choose to fear God alone. He needs to be the only one you are out to please.

I believe I'm addressing what you may be facing right now. You may be born again, you may have been filled with the Holy Spirit, but you don't seek the honor that comes from God alone. If you're being honest, you know you compromise your faith. Maybe you refuse to speak out and stand up because it might cost you the acceptance of people, a raise at your job, your popularity in the bowling league, or whatever else is important to you. This stops you from being a strong believer. I'm not trying to hurt your feelings; I'm saying these things to enlighten you and encourage you to be like Daniel and his three friends.

God built us with a desire to be loved. The majority of people try to satisfy this desire by seeking acceptance from as many people as possible, following the crowd through the broad gate that leads to destruction rather than finding the narrow gate leading to life (Matt. 7:13-14). Christians who prioritize being accepted by everyone will eventually compromise in certain areas. That's why you must be bold enough not to follow the crowd. If you do that, then you'll be strong in faith.

When your identity is in God, when you've purposed not to compromise, you need boldness that will cause you to stand up in the face of adversity. When you do this, you won't worry about what people will say. This is part of what it takes to have an excellent spirit, and God promotes that. I'm not proclaiming that I've done everything perfectly, but I have done these things to a degree. I'm seeking to do it better all the time. You must be bold enough to stand up and speak the truth regardless of what it costs you.

Daniel in the Lions' Den

Let me illustrate what boldness looked like in the life of Daniel. After the Babylonian empire fell to the Persian empire, he began serving under King Darius. He might have been ninety years old (or older) at this time, yet he still had favor with man. Look at these verses in Daniel 6:

> *It pleased Darius to set over the kingdom an hundred and twenty princes, which should be over the whole kingdom; And over these three presidents; of whom Daniel was first: that the princes might give*

accounts unto them, and the king should have no damage. Then this Daniel was preferred above the presidents and princes, because an excellent spirit was in him; and the king thought to set him over the whole realm.

Daniel 6:1-3

Daniel, a non-Persian, was placed in charge of the entire Persian kingdom—the largest empire that had ever existed in Daniel's day. What reason does Scripture give for this happening? Because he had an excellent spirit!

Then the princes and other presidents tried to find something against Daniel (Dan. 6:4). He hadn't done anything to cause this; it was just jealousy on their part. They reasoned amongst themselves and said,

We shall not find any occasion against this Daniel, except we find it against him concerning the law of his God.

Daniel 6:5

Imagine if every one of us demonstrated such unwavering commitment to God's calling that even our enemies couldn't find fault. That's the way it ought to be. This was actually a tremendous compliment. When we're drawing persecution from the enemy, that means we're running against him. We're doing something right. But if we never run into the devil, it's because we're heading in the same direction.

Because these evil men knew that Daniel was a man of integrity, they planned to use that against him. It was easier for them to try to drag him down to their level than to rise to his. They would do this by playing to King Darius's ego. They knew they could fool him into making a decree that all people should pray to him or be put to death. Now, of course, Daniel—having a close relationship with God, knowing his identity, not being willing to compromise—refused to comply. But here's what he did that very few are willing to do:

> *Now when Daniel knew that the writing was signed, he went into his house; and his windows being open in his chamber toward Jerusalem, he kneeled upon his knees three times a day, and prayed, and gave thanks before his God, as he did aforetime.*

> Daniel 6:10

Daniel knew that according to the writing, or decree, he would be thrown into a den of lions if he prayed to God. He could have prayed silently in his heart, or with his windows closed. God would have heard him. But Daniel opened his windows to make sure everyone could see him kneeling and praying toward Jerusalem three times a day, just the way he had always done. It was a deliberate act of boldness. He knew his life would be on the line. This is important to understand when we're talking about boldness.

When an ungodly command is issued to be obeyed under penalty of death, most people wouldn't have the backbone to stand for godliness. "What's the alternative?" someone will ask, "It sounds like you're promoting anarchy." I am not promoting anarchy, but I am saying that there is a place for civil disobedience. You need this kind of boldness in order to have an excellent spirit. Again, this is a choice.

If you say, "But I don't want people to be offended by my faith. I'll just hide what I believe and not stand for truth," God will not promote you. He is looking for people like Daniel who, even when it's against the law to obey Him, even when it's against public opinion, even if costs them something, will stand for who He made them to be. These are people who will stand for the truth, and they will speak the truth in love (Eph. 4:15). I'm not talking about having a bad attitude or disposition. Boldness is not permission to be a jerk in the name of Christ. Some people use the Word of God like a club to beat people over the head. That's mean-spiritedness. However, you should be able to tell them the truth out of a heart of love. It's the truth that sets people free (John 8:32).

If you say, "But I do love them. That's why I'm not going to say anything," you don't have an excellent spirit. The Scripture doesn't say that love sets people free. You need to decide you love people enough to tell them the truth. You have to realize that it's only the truth people *know* that will set them free. If you're not bold enough to tell them, it's because you love yourself more than you love them. It's because you're worried about the rejection, the persecution, and the criticism that might come against you. I encourage you to learn from Daniel's example and begin to start speaking out.

To continue the story, the evil presidents and princes came before the king to inform him that Daniel had defied his decree to pray only to him:

Then they came near, and spake before the king concerning the king's decree; Hast thou not signed a decree, that every man that shall ask a petition *of any God or man within thirty days, save of thee, O king, shall be cast into the den of lions? The king answered and said, The thing* is *true, according to the law of the Medes and Persians, which altereth not. Then answered they and said before the king, That Daniel, which* is *of the children of the captivity of Judah, regardeth not thee, O king, nor the decree that thou hast signed, but maketh his petition three times a day. Then the king, when he heard* these *words, was sore displeased with himself, and set* his *heart on Daniel to deliver him: and he laboured till the going down of the sun to deliver him.*

Daniel 6:12-14

In other words, despite his ego, despite this irreversible decree that he had set forth, King Darius had such value for Daniel that he wanted to preserve his life. That's favor! This was because of Daniel's excellent spirit. But even though he was displeased with himself for falling into the trap set by these wicked men, the king had to honor his decree to have Daniel arrested and thrown in a lions' den. However, Darius spoke blessings upon Daniel, that God would preserve his life (Dan. 6:16). As a matter of fact, the king didn't sleep all night! At sunlight, he went quickly to see if Daniel had survived:

> *And when he came to the den, he cried with a lamentable voice unto Daniel:* and *the king spake and said to Daniel, O Daniel, servant of the living God, is thy God, whom thou servest continually, able to deliver thee from the lions? Then said Daniel unto the king, O king, live for ever. My God hath sent his angel, and hath shut the lions' mouths, that they have not hurt me: forasmuch as before him innocency was found in me; and also before thee, O king, have I done no hurt.*

> Daniel 6:20-22

Do you see how Daniel's boldness to stand up for truth not only gave him favor but also saved him from the mouths of these lions? Of course, you would love to have Daniel's results, but are you willing to go through what he went through to get it? To see God do great miracles for you, you must find your true identity in the Lord, refuse to compromise, and be bold. Then you'll be walking in a spirit of excellence, and God will promote you.

Chapter 4

Humbly Trust

Humility is the fourth quality of an excellent spirit. This is mentioned in many places in Scripture, not just the stories of Daniel and his friends.

If you think that you are a self-made man or woman and that you can do things on your own, you are heading for disaster. God didn't make you to run your own life. Pride goes before destruction and a haughty spirit before a fall (Prov. 16:18).

If you are all wrapped up in yourself, you make a very small package. Pride is a characteristic of a person who does *not* have an excellent spirit. Even if you're a ten-talent person (see Matt. 25:14-30), or naturally beautiful, and you have everything others struggle to have—you need to humble yourself. Recognize that every one of those gifts and talents came from God (1 Cor. 4:7; James 1:17). To walk in humility, as it relates to an excellent spirit, you must recognize that God is the source of everything good in your life.

Humility doesn't mean you're weak. It doesn't mean that if you have a nice operatic voice, you should tell people, "Well, I don't have much of a voice, but the Word says to make a joyful noise unto the Lord. You all pray for me today." That's not a humble person; that's just a religious con. There's nothing wrong with you saying that you've got a great voice if you don't take the credit for yourself. A humble person will acknowledge God and give Him all the glory.

Respond to God's Ability

Did you know that if you are overwhelmed with bearing the burden of life's responsibilities, you are not a humble person? That may be a brand-new wrinkle in your brain, but it's the truth. Most people think that pride is exalting yourself and thinking you're better than everybody else. That is one manifestation of pride, but pride also includes taking on the responsibility of making things happen. If you think of yourself as the source, that's pride. If you feel you have to make a living, be the protector of your family, and fix everything all on your own, you're operating in pride. Look at 1 Peter 5:6-7:

> *Humble yourselves therefore under the mighty hand*
> *of God, that he may exalt you in due time: Casting*
> *all your care upon him; for he careth for you.*

People often take "*casting all your care*" on the Lord out of context. They totally miss that this is talking about humbling yourself. You'll notice that 1 Peter 5:6 ends with a colon, not a period. That means that humbling yourself is tied to what comes next. This is saying that the way you humble yourself is by casting your care on the Lord, knowing that He cares for you!

When you're humble, you pray, "Father, this problem is Your responsibility. I'm giving it to You." You need to make sure you're doing what He told you to do and you're not trying to get God to subsidize your evil behavior or your own personal plans. But when you stop taking responsibility and start responding to *His* ability, you are a humble person. Humility is God-dependence instead of self-dependence. Instead of trusting in yourself, humility is letting God run your life and work things out. The Bible says,

> O Lord, I know that the way of man is not in him-self: it is not in man that walketh to direct his steps.
>
> Jeremiah 10:23

Your steps are to be ordered of the Lord (Ps. 37:23), so when you stop trusting yourself and start trusting God, then you're walking in humility.

Grace to the Humble

Did you know that God Himself is humble? Jesus said,

> Come unto me, all ye that labour and are heavy laden, and I will give you rest. Take my yoke upon you, and learn of me; for I am meek and lowly in heart: and ye shall find rest unto your souls.
>
> Matt. 11:28-29

This was God in the flesh, and He said, "I am meek and lowly in heart." Most people would never put "God" and "humble" in the same sentence. They only think of God as being almighty and all-knowing. But God is humble. He is not a self-promoting, egotistical God. And because God is humble, He resists things that aren't like Him:

God resisteth the proud, and giveth grace to the humble.

1 Peter 5:5b

If we're in pride, I don't believe that God resists us by taking a personal vendetta against us; however, God's kingdom is built on humility. It's His nature and His character to not promote people who are the antithesis of Him. He won't do it. God will promote people who have His heart.

To have an excellent spirit, you need to humble yourself. You need to cast your care over on the Lord and turn your life over to Him. Let God be the source of everything you need. Start responding to His ability instead of trusting in your own.

Conclusion

I hope what I've shared about an excellent spirit has ministered to you! It is so important that you begin to walk in these things. God wants to promote you. You can go as high as you want to go. The sky is the limit! But God is only going to promote those who have an excellent spirit.

I encourage you to start where you are. Whatever God has called you to do, do it with excellence. If you're praying for a better car, yet you've trashed the one you've got, that is not a spirit of excellence. You must first take care of what He has already given you, and then He will bless you with more. You might be believing God for a new place to live, and yet you're not being a good steward of the home you've got. Why would God give you something brand new if you're going to trash that one too? Someone might be thinking, *If I had something better, I'd take care of it!* That's not the principle that the Lord teaches in the Word. If you aren't faithful in that which is little, who is going to commit to your trust greater riches (Luke 16:10-11)?

Now, God loves you. He wants to bless you. He loves you so much that He would love to see you get this spirit of excellence. Start today by saying, "I'm going to do the best I possibly can with what I have. I may not have much right now, but I'm going to take care of it."

The spirit of excellence is in short supply today. Most people shoot at nothing and hit it every time. That is not what God made you for. You don't have to live a mediocre life. God made you to be exceptional in every way! The path to promotion is just as important as the promotion itself. It starts with developing an excellent spirit. To do that you must have a close relationship with God and establish your identity in Him, hold on to your identity by refusing to compromise who you are, be bold and willing to take a stand without backing down, and be humble by relying on God's ability instead of your own.

It doesn't matter the limitations you perceive—your race, gender, or education. If you possess the excellent spirit that Daniel and his friends had, God will promote you, just as He did them. He is no respecter of persons (Acts 10:34 and Rom. 2:11).

I believe that God has spoken to you through what I've shared in this booklet. You need to respond. Make the decision today to begin walking in a spirit of excellence, and it will only be a matter of time before you experience promotion. I guarantee it!

FURTHER STUDY

If you enjoyed this booklet and would like to learn more about some of the things I've shared, I suggest my teachings:

1. *Lessons from Joseph*
2. *Ten Godly Leadership Essentials*
3. *Self-Centeredness: The Source of All Grief*

These teachings are available for free at **awmi.net**, or they can be purchased at **awmi.net/store**.

Receive Jesus as
Your Savior

Choosing to receive Jesus Christ as your Lord and Savior is the most important decision you'll ever make!

God's Word promises, *"That if thou shalt confess with thy mouth the Lord Jesus, and shalt believe in thine heart that God hath raised him from the dead, thou shalt be saved. For with the heart man believeth unto righteousness; and with the mouth confession is made unto salvation"* (Rom. 10:9–10). *"For whosoever shall call upon the name of the Lord shall be saved"* (Rom. 10:13). By His grace, God has already done everything to provide salvation. Your part is simply to believe and receive.

Pray out loud: "Jesus, I acknowledge that I've sinned and need to receive what you did for the forgiveness of my sins. I confess that You are my Lord and Savior. I believe in my heart that God raised You from the dead. By faith in Your Word, I receive salvation now. Thank You for saving me."

The very moment you commit your life to Jesus Christ, the truth of His Word instantly comes to pass in your spirit. Now that you're born again, there's a brand-new you!

Please contact us and let us know that you've prayed to receive Jesus as your Savior. We'd like to send you some free materials to help you on your new journey. Call our Helpline: **719-635-1111** (available 24 hours a day, seven days a week) to speak to a staff member who is here to help you understand and grow in your new relationship with the Lord.

Welcome to your new life!

Receive
the Holy Spirit

A s His child, your loving heavenly Father wants to give you the supernatural power you need to live a new life. *"For every one that asketh receiveth; and he that seeketh findeth; and to him that knocketh it shall be opened...how much more shall* your *heavenly Father give the Holy Spirit to them that ask him?"* (Luke 11:10–13).

All you have to do is ask, believe, and receive!

Pray this: "Father, I recognize my need for Your power to live a new life. Please fill me with Your Holy Spirit. By faith, I receive it right now. Thank You for baptizing me. Holy Spirit, You are welcome in my life."

Some syllables from a language you don't recognize will rise up from your heart to your mouth (1 Cor. 14:14). As you speak them out loud by faith, you're releasing God's power from within and building yourself up in the spirit (1 Cor. 14:4). You can do this whenever and wherever you like.

It doesn't really matter whether you felt anything or not when you prayed to receive the Lord and His Spirit. If you believed in your heart that you received, then God's Word promises you did. *"Therefore I say unto you, What things soever ye desire, when ye pray, believe that ye receive them, and ye shall have them"* (Mark 11:24). God always honors His Word—believe it!

We would like to rejoice with you, pray with you, and answer any questions to help you understand more fully what has taken place in your life!

Please contact us to let us know that you've prayed to be filled with the Holy Spirit and to request the book *The New You & the Holy Spirit.* This book will explain in more detail about the benefits of being filled with the Holy Spirit and speaking in tongues. Call our Helpline: **719-635-1111** (available 24 hours a day, seven days a week).

Call for Prayer

I f you need prayer for any reason, you can call our Helpline, 24 hours a day, seven days a week at **719-635-1111**. A trained prayer minister will answer your call and pray with you.

Every day, we receive testimonies of healings and other miracles from our Helpline, and we are ministering God's nearly-too-good-to-be-true message of the Gospel to more people than ever. So, I encourage you to call today!

About the Author

Andrew Wommack's life was forever changed the moment he encountered the supernatural love of God on March 23, 1968. As a renowned Bible teacher and author, Andrew has made it his mission to change the way the world sees God.

Andrew's vision is to go as far and deep with the Gospel as possible. His message goes far through the *Gospel Truth* television program, which is available to over half the world's population. The message goes deep through discipleship at Charis Bible College, headquartered in Woodland Park, Colorado. Founded in 1994, Charis has campuses across the United States and around the globe.

Andrew also has an extensive library of teaching materials in print, audio, and video. More than 200,000 hours of free teachings can be accessed at **awmi.net**.

Contact Information

Andrew Wommack Ministries, Inc.

PO Box 3333
Colorado Springs, CO 80934-3333
info@awmi.net
awmi.net

Helpline: 719-635-1111 (available 24/7)

Charis Bible College

info@charisbiblecollege.org
844-360-9577
CharisBibleCollege.org

For a complete list of all of our offices,
visit **awmi.net/contact-us**.

Connect with us on social media.

Andrew's
LIVING
COMMENTARY
BIBLE SOFTWARE

Andrew Wommack's *Living Commentary* Bible study software is a user-friendly, downloadable program. It's like reading the Bible with Andrew at your side, sharing his revelation with you verse by verse.

Main features:

- Bible study software with a grace-and-faith perspective
- Over 26,000 notes by Andrew on verses from Genesis through Revelation
- *Matthew Henry's Concise Commentary*
- 12 Bible versions
- 2 concordances: *Englishman's Concordance* and *Strong's Concordance*
- 2 dictionaries: *Collaborative International Dictionary* and *Holman's Dictionary*
- Atlas with biblical maps
- Bible and *Living Commentary* statistics
- Quick navigation, including history of verses
- Robust search capabilities (for the Bible and Andrew's notes)
- "Living" (i.e., constantly updated and expanding)
- Ability to create personal notes

Whether you're new to studying the Bible or a seasoned Bible scholar, you'll gain a deeper revelation of the Word from a grace-and-faith perspective.

Purchase Andrew's *Living Commentary* today at **awmi.net/living**, and grow in the Word with Andrew.

Item code: 8350

ANDREW WOMMACK MINISTRIES

Made in the USA
Middletown, DE
24 August 2024